Lotty can see a ship in the tub.

Lotty jumps in the tub to play with the ship.

Lotty has fun in the tub with the ship.

Kevin jumps in the tub to play with the ship.

Crack! Oh no! The tub splits. Splash!

Splash! Bump!
Lotty is flat on the path.

Splash! Bump! Kevin is on the top of Lotty.

Oh no! Kevin and Lotty are on the ship.